I0163096

Fire in My Bones

Created by God
Written by Charles C. Smith, Jr.

MICK ART
PRODUCTIONS LLC
PUBLISHING

The author has represented and warranted full ownership and/or legal right to publish all the materials in this book.

Fire in My Bones
All Rights Reserved Copyright © 2019 Charles C. Smith, Jr.
This book may not be reproduced, transmitted, or stored in whole or in part by any means, including graphics, electronic, or mechanical without the express written consent of the publisher except in the case of brief quotations embodied in critical articles and reviews.

ISBN: 978-1-948508-04-9

Published by
Mick Art Productions, LLC
www.mickartproductions.com
PRINTED IN THE UNITED STATES OF AMERICA

Hello,

As you read this book, I pray that every revelation that God opens up to you will motivate you to desire much more of Him, His will, plan, presence, spirit, and ways. God blessed me to grow in multiple ways myself as He used me to write this life altering message to all who trust and believe in Him, and even those who do not. Please don't just read these words. Allow them to live in, with, and through you every second of your life! Expect for God to do some amazing things! Expect Him to move fear, move judgment, move doubt, move hurt, move habits, move conditioning, and to ignite His spirit in you!

Tell God: "I want to feel the fire in my bones!"

Charles C. Smith Jr.

Dedication

I dedicate this book to my mother, Olevia Smith, and to all the people I love.

Mom, you're truly an amazing woman! You have a heart that loves beyond measure and a strength that only God could have given you! I can use every positive word or expression that is available to man to tell about your kind of love and I would still need more. So I'll just say that you'll never truly understand how many people have been impacted by God's love living through you! I love and respect you so very much!

Thank you, Mom!

To those I love,

In life, we will be challenged by many situations, trials, and tribulations. If we find our strength in God, we will not be over taken by any of them. God has been, is, and will always be the answer to everything we encounter! Get close to Him, live close to Him, and desire more of Him every day that He gives you breath!

I love you and God bless and keep all of you!

Table of Content

Introduction

In the Bible, in the book of Jeremiah, God's prophet, Jeremiah had to minister and deliver God's harsh message to Pashhur (the official in charge of the temple of the LORD). Because of the harsh message, Jeremiah was beaten and jailed by Pashhur. He was also mocked and ridiculed by other people. This torture caused Jeremiah to want to quit his ministry and not speak for God, anymore. In Jeremiah 20:7-8, you'll see how Jeremiah was discouraged.

Jeremiah 19:14-15 & 20:1-9 (NIV)

The Word of God to Pashhur

14 Jeremiah then returned from Topheth, where the LORD had sent him to prophesy, and stood in the court of the LORD's temple and said to all the people, 15 "This is what the LORD Almighty, the God of Israel, says: 'Listen! I am going to bring on this city and all the villages around it every disaster I pronounced against them because they were stiff-necked and would not listen to my words.'"

Jeremiah and Pashhur

20 When the priest Pashhur son of Immer, the official in charge of the temple of the LORD, heard Jeremiah prophesying these things, 2 he had Jeremiah the prophet beaten and put in the stocks at the Upper Gate of Benjamin at the LORD's temple. 3 The next day, when Pashhur released him from the stocks, Jeremiah said to him, "The LORD's name for you is not Pashhur, but Terror on Every Side. 4 For this is what the LORD says: 'I will make you a terror to yourself and to all your friends; with your own eyes you will see them fall by the sword of their enemies. I will give all Judah into the hands of the king of Babylon, who will carry them away to Babylon or put them to the sword. 5 I will deliver all the wealth of this city into the hands of their enemies—all its products, all its valuables and all the treasures of the kings of Judah. They will take it away as plunder and carry it off to Babylon. 6 And you, Pashhur, and all who live in your house will go into exile to Babylon.

There you will die and be buried, you and all your friends to whom you have prophesied lies."

Jeremiah's Complaint

7 You deceived me, LORD, and I was deceived; you overpowered me and prevailed. I am ridiculed all day long; everyone mocks me. 8 Whenever I speak, I cry out proclaiming violence and destruction. So the Word of the LORD has brought me insult and reproach all day long. 9 But if I say, "I will not mention His word or speak any more in His name," His Word is in my heart like a fire, a fire shut up in my bones. I am weary of holding it in; indeed, I cannot.

Jeremiah knew that God's Word was rooted deep in his heart and that he couldn't hold back from speaking it. Jeremiah states in verse 20:9 "His word is in my heart like a fire, a fire shut up in my bones; I am weary of holding it in; indeed, I cannot." Jeremiah couldn't hold back from doing what God had created and chose Him to do!

I pray this book will inspire you to thirst for God's presence, Word, and Will, so much that you'll tell God,

"I WANT TO FEEL THE FIRE IN MY BONES!"

Chapter 1
Change What You Believe About Yourself!

Change your perception!

When we look at ourselves, our perception of who we are is usually based on how we compare to others, in some way. We compare ourselves to siblings, other family members, people from school, work, teams, friends, and people from church, etc. So, we gauge our lives by how we compare to these other people and our perception of their lives, successes, and failures. If we believe they are doing better/worse at something that we are striving to accomplish, we see ourselves as less than or as better than them. I have been told and have told others that perception is reality to the person that has the perception! I believe this is very true; we have all responded with decisions, choices, actions, and reactions to our perception of what we experience. So, that means that what we believe about ourselves is going to be based on what perception we choose to accept as our truth.

When I was a teenager, I loved playing basketball; I still do. However, when I was younger, my older brother (Frenchie L. Lane) was one of the best players I had ever seen on the court. I never saw him lose in a one-on-one game; I wanted to be as good as him. However, I didn't have the natural abilities that he had on the court. I lacked confidence in myself, because of it. One day on the court a kid my age and my brother's friend were talking smack about this kid being better than me at basketball. My brother quickly and proudly said, "he can beat him, and I'll bet you $20 he'll win." I said to my brother, "I can't beat him, he's better than me, he's faster, dribbles, and shoots better than me." But, my brother pulled me to the side and said, "you shoot just as good, you're just as fast, you hustle, and you play good defense. You Can Beat Him!" That moment changed what I believed about myself. I got on the court with a new confidence, because the person I looked up to told me I was good enough to do it and I won 2 games out 3. God had already given me the ability; I didn't see it, so I didn't believe it, but God was moving in my life! Through my brother, God showed me His perception of me and the talents He had given me! My brother later told me that he knew I would win, so he bet $20 he didn't have! Wow, the crazy situations siblings will get you into!!!!

I chose to believe God's perception of me through my brother! What will you choose will you believe your perception, Satan's perception, or God's perception of you? Just know that Satan's perception of you will be deceptive, negative, and discouraging, in order to trap you in unbelief!

But, if you're choosing to believe God's perception of you, you'll have to change what you believe about yourself! To change what you believe about yourself, you have to seek, desire, trust, and thirst for more of God and what He says! Tell God: "I want to feel the fire in my bones!"

At this point, you may be questioning what you believe about yourself, or maybe good with what you believe about yourself. If you're asking yourself what do I believe about myself, it is the perfect time to find out what God says about you! If you're among those who are good with what you believe about yourself, here are some questions,

What do you fear failing at?
What do you fear people knowing about you?
What do you fear doing or not doing?
Whose approval are you afraid of losing or not having?
What situations do you fear being in or not getting out of?
What person or people do you fear leaving your life?

We could continue with so many other fears that we all have that affect what we believe about ourselves. We have to be aware of what we're allowing to help create our perception of ourselves. God says that He is not the author of fear, so when we allow fear to take part in shaping our perception of what we're created to do, we fear the world's perception of failure. So I ask, are you okay with accepting that you're afraid? If not, you have to change what you believe about yourself and trust God's perception of failure. You see, the world says that if you attempt to accomplish something and you don't, you have failed! But with God, if you try and don't accomplish it, it's a lesson and His testimony helping you move toward being who God says you are! There is no failure in trusting God; the only way you experience failure is by not trusting God! Failing to trust God will allow fear to stop you from moving, and you will fail! Fear will then hold you hostage whenever God tells you to move! Don't be held hostage; change what you believe about yourself!

Conquer the doubt!

Your fears will help to shape your doubt. You'll find yourself doubting that God will use your gifts, talents, and abilities that He's given you, or you won't believe He's given you gifts, talents, and abilities. When doubt has found its way into your mind, it will cause you to ignore God's guidance and vision for you. You know, God shows you how, when, where, and who, but you listen to the doubt that you have. What does doubt say? It says not you, you didn't hear clearly, that wasn't God, those are your thoughts, I'm not ready, I'm uncomfortable, etc. Then, at the same time, Satan influences certain people that are around you to speak doubt into your life, as well. If your foundation is not in what God has said about you and that He has a plan for your life, a plan to prepare you, you will accept what doubt has to say! You will then choose not to move when God says move, or will move when God says be still! Either way, you find yourself out of the will of God. You may even blame God for the results of your choice; which, is exactly what Satan will use to continue to add bricks to your wall of doubt about yourself and God! Listen, never doubt that God has chosen you for His will, purpose, and plan to reach people. See yourself through God. You have to change what you believe about yourself! Tell God: "I want to feel the fire in my bones!"

You have to conquer doubt, or you will see yourself as unable, unqualified, and unworthy to be used by God. This has, is, and will happen to so many of us as we learn how to live for Christ. The world has conditioned us to believe in what the world says about being effective or successful in life. So, we carry this same mindset into our living for God. If we see ourselves as being less of a speaker, teacher, Bible student, singer, musician, prayer, churchgoer, etc. We can begin to think we are unable, unqualified, and unworthy of God's purpose. Here's a question, what enables, qualifies, and makes you worthy for God's purpose?

God makes the choice!

A man or woman cannot determine if you're able to be used by God. If a man or woman tries to dictate how God is going to use you, they are out of order. God created you for His purpose and He knows the full plan and purpose for your life. God can and will use others to teach and guide you, according to His will! You have to spend time with Him, so that you know the difference between when people are imposing their will onto you, instead of God's will. You don't need man's approval to be used by God.

Ephesians 4:7 "God's favor has been given to us. It was measured out to us by Christ who gave it."

So, if Christ gave you His measure of favor, that would mean that He chose to give you His approval to live out that favor that is given to you. If you have been chosen by God, no one on this earth has the power to change His mind about choosing you! Because God created you and you have accepted Christ as your savior, you have already been stamped able, qualified, and worthy for God's purpose and plan for your life. To answer the question, what enables, qualifies, and makes you worthy for God's purpose and plans, the answer is Christ! In the world people value fame, wealth and power. That is why we feel we have to be known by the world to be heard, so, you must change what you believe about yourself!

Dismiss the negativity!

Don't allow the negativity to live in you; dismiss it! Trust in what God says about you to conquer feeling and thinking you're unable, unqualified, and unworthy for God's purpose and plan! If you allow negativity to live in you, you can begin to feel that you have no purpose and that people don't see your worth. You may start to feel and think that you have nothing to give, are unnoticed, unknown, lonely, and devalued. This is also a trick of the Devil. The more you feel unknown or devalued, the more you question your existence. Don't accept or allow this mindset to settle in your spirit; dismiss the negativity. You have to change what you believe about yourself! God created you, and He cherishes everyone He created. That alone says you have a wealth of value in what God created you to be! This world doesn't have to acknowledge who God says you are for it to be true; it is true simply because God said it! In this world, people value fame, wealth, and power. That is why we feel we have been known by the world to be heard, but we're wrong in this thought process. The world values one person more than another; God doesn't! God's Word says that God created man in His image, so how can a person God created in His likeness be less than any other person God created? It is not possible, in God's eyes. The sins we commit have to be forgiven through Christ; however, God's love and how He values us doesn't change! If you feel or think that you have nothing to give or that you're unnoticed, unknown, lonely and devalued; dismiss that negativity! You have to change what you believe about yourself! Choose to believe that you're a child of God; created, saved, justified, favored, and valued by God! You are precisely what God created you to be. You have to choose to live it out by faith!

I am a father of four handsome young men (Charles Smith III, Ryan King, Victor Smith, and Daimon Washington) and two beautiful young women (Takeisha Smith and Lauryn Smith)! I have six children with five different mothers. Okay, now pick your jaws up! That is the usual response I get from people and have for years. The second thought is what kind of father is he? I admit, this was and is a challenging life to live, and there have been many things that have been said and done to affect what I believed about myself, as a father and a man. My relationship is different with each one of my children. Several are challenging because of what has been said or done, and others are great, because of what has been heard and accepted. However, my love is the same for each of them! God helped me to understand that sharing His love with them is what makes me a great father, not what people think or believe! That gave me the strength and confidence to be my best, no matter what was said or done or how little I had to offer.

I'm the perfect ME! No one else can be me, speak like ME, look like ME, use their talents like ME, love like ME, care like Me, give like ME, serve like ME, praise like ME, worship like ME, trust like ME, learn like ME or live like ME! God created me just the way I am! Sin, and not following God with my choices, creates my flaws. The world says being like the world is the perfect person to be. However, God made Me according to His purpose, plan, and His perception of who I am. So, that makes ME the only ME God has made. Therefore, I'm the perfect ME created by God.

GOD IS MISTAKE FREE!!!!

Just be who God says you are, not what or who others say you should be! Change what you believe about yourself!

TELL GOD: "I WANT TO FEEL THE FIRE IN MY BONES!"

You are God's child; you're royalty! You are not less than any other man! You are in God's likeness!

Chapter 2
Control Your Circle!

Control who you allow in your circle!

When you desire to be what God created you to be and do, you have to be mindful of what and who you entertain. We all have people who come into our lives and seem to be nice. They may know someone we know; they've known our family, because of work, because of school, or because of our children, etc. How often do we ask God or test them by the Word of God before letting them in? Our spiritual lives are impacted by the people we allow to be in our circle. At times, we will take advice from them, follow their lead, we go where they go, and we also will react the way they react. We will allow them to influence us in our everyday life! We should always examine our interaction with our circle. You may find that the spirit in some of the people in your circle doesn't edify or encourage your relationship with God. You will need to control who you allow in!

If we aren't careful, we can find ourselves taking advice from or following the wrong spirit. We have to trust in the spirit of God and what it reveals to us about the people around us. You don't have to allow them to influence your life. But, you do have to control your circle and what influences you. Jesus chose each one of His disciples; they didn't choose to be disciples on their own! You see, Jesus knew the heart of each man He chose and their purpose in fulfilling God's plan. It is the same today in our lives; God knows who, when, why, where, and how to place the right people in our circle. So, you have to trust God's guidance as you focus on controlling your circle and decide to chase after the spirit of God! Tell God: "I want to feel the fire in my bones!"

Control what you accept from your circle!

Controlling your circle is not a simple task. You have to control who you'll allow in and what you'll accept from them. Just because we allow someone in our circle doesn't mean we have to accept everything they bring. We must be in prayer and in the Word of God, so that we know what to dismiss. Some people will tell you that God told them to say or do things; you have to test it against God's Word. That means you have to spend time with God in His Word, so that you have it in you. So that, with prayer and the Word of God living in you, you will recognize what is not of God. Jesus put this on display when He corrected the spirit in Peter.

Matthew 16:23 NIV "Jesus turned and said to Peter, "Get behind me, Satan! You are a stumbling block to me; you do not have in mind the concerns of God, but merely human concerns."

Jesus knew He had to control what He accepted from His circle! However, there will be times when God has chosen to allow things to happen for His purpose in your life. You may find yourself in a situation that doesn't feel or look good, but it's in God's plan. In these moments, you have to trust in God's promise to never leave you and to finish the work He started in you. Jesus did this when he called out Judas at the last supper.

Matthew 26:23-25 (NIV) 23 Jesus replied, "The one who has dipped his hand into the bowl with me will betray me. 24 The Son of Man will go just as it is written about him. But woe to that man who betrays the Son of Man! It would be better for him if he had not been born." 25 Then Judas, the one who would betray him, said, "Surely you don't mean me, Rabbi?" Jesus answered, "You have said so."

Jesus chose to accept God's plan and the betrayal from His circle. We also have to trust God to reveal what to accept as His plan! Tell God: "I want to feel the fire in my bones!"

Control how you react to your circle!

As you work to control your circle, you must be aware of how you react to them. We cannot control what they chose to do, but we can control how we choose to react to it! For example, you may have people tell you that they support you and that they have your back. But when you need them most, they find reasons not to be or do what they told you they would be or do. You may not like what happens, but you can choose to hold them accountable in God's love. Jesus did this in the garden of Gethsemane.

Matthew 36:38 & 40 (NIV), 38 Then He said to them, "My soul is overwhelmed with sorrow to the point of death. Stay here and keep watch with me." 40 Then he returned to His disciples and found them sleeping. "Couldn't you men keep watch with me for one hour?" He asked Peter. 41 "Watch and pray so that you will not fall into temptation. The spirit is willing, but the flesh is weak."

Jesus didn't get angry, because He understood who He was dealing with. He knew how to control how He reacted to His circle. There will be times when other people won't be able to do what your faith leads you to do. You may be the more spiritually mature person in your circle, so you have to control how you react to them! Doing this will also serve as the living testimony of your faith. God tells us, who believe in Christ, to be a living example of His Word. So, choose to control how you react to your circle and choose to be God's example. Tell God: "I want to feel the fire in my bones!"

Please remember this, when you choose to really seek God, the Devil will get busy! You now have a target on your back for the Devil's archery practice, and arrows will keep coming! The purpose of these arrows is to discourage you from living out your decision. However, you have a promise from Christ that none of the Devil's attacks will prevail!

Jesus says in Luke 10:19,19 I have given you authority to trample on snakes and scorpions and to overcome all the power of the enemy; nothing will harm you.

The Devil will use whoever will make themselves available to be used by him. They may not even realize they have given themselves over to be used to discourage you. This is why you have to control how you react to your circle and respond through the Holy Spirit; rather, than self. Your reaction to God's spirit will be God's testimony and your living example of Christ.

I saw this take place with my youngest daughter, Lauryn, when she was diagnosed with cancer at sixteen. Lauryn maintained a strong faith that God was using her through this battle with cancer. Her friends were upset, sad, and some cried when they would speak with her about her situation. I remember her telling me that she told her friends she doesn't need for them to be sad. She told them she has faith and God is using her for His testimony, and that she encouraged them to believe as well. God was doing exactly what she said; He healed her from cancer and made her His testimony! Her reacting in faith moved others to desire a stronger faith and a closer relationship with God!

For some people, they can only see Christ when Christ is living through you. Use the Holy Spirit to control how you react to your circle and choose to be God's testimony.

TELL GOD: "I WANT TO FEEL THE FIRE IN MY BONES!"

You can be influenced! The question is who or what will you allow to influence you? Choose God's influence.

Chapter 3
Challenge Where You Are!

Acknowledge where you are!

To challenge where you are, you have to know, understand, and acknowledge where you are. This means you have to take a look at yourself and be honest with yourself and God about what you see. The purpose of this is not to show God where you are with Him; it's so that you realize where you are in Him; God already knows! God has always pushed His children to look at their condition from the beginning of His creating us; he did it with Adam in the Garden of Eden.

Genesis 3:8-12 (NIV), 8 Then the man and his wife heard the sound of the LORD God as he was walking in the garden in the cool of the day, and they hid from the LORD God among the trees of the garden. 9 But the LORD God called to the man, "Where are you?" 10 He answered, "I heard you in the garden, and I was afraid because I was naked; so I hid." 11 And he said, "Who told you that you were naked? Have you eaten from the tree that I commanded you not to eat from?" 12 The man said, "The woman you put here with me—she gave me some fruit from the tree, and I ate it."

God was not asking Adam where he was because He didn't know, He was asking because He wanted Adam to acknowledge the condition he was now in! When Adam understood his condition, he understood the necessity to be obedient to God. Once you know where you are in God, you know your obedience to God, if you're honest! Remember this, there is no room for anyone to pass judgment on your obedience to God; we all fall short in our obedience! However, you can acknowledge where you are and challenge where you are. Surrender to God and He will change where you are; you cannot do it without God! Adam and Eve still had to live out the results of their choice in the Garden of Eden. But, God was still there, God was still God in their lives, just as He is today in our lives as we fall short. You have to accept and acknowledge your condition and challenge where you are by surrendering to God, minute by minute! Tell God: "I want to feel the fire in my bones!"

Surrender to God!

Surrendering to God is a constant challenge when we are living in a world where the actions of people are guided by selfish gain, self-glorification, and disbelief in God. In this world, what is right in God is seen as wrong, and what is wrong in the world is seen as right. Listen, just because the majority agrees doesn't make it right. If it doesn't align with God's Word, what you have is a lot of people agreeing with the wrong! If you find yourself following the choices of the majority; instead, of standing in God, you need to challenge where you are! Going along with the crowd seems to be the easier route because you think you will avoid conflict. However, if you have accepted Christ in your life, you cannot avoid conflict with the world! Living for God should take us out of our comfort zone, because we can no longer live as the world lives. Being in your comfort zone can hold your ministry hostage, if you refused to leave where you are. You may not feel or be strong enough to walk away from people, things, and situations in your life and you will need for God to intervene. Sometimes, God will move things out of your life gradually, and at other times He will snatch you or it out, immediately. Either way, you have to surrender to God and let Him take you away from it or take it away from you! Once God has moved you or it, DO NOT go back to it, or let it back into your life! There will be many times when people won't like you standing on God's Word, and it will cause conflict. It happened in the Bible constantly, even to the point where God's people were beaten, imprisoned, and even killed. We're living in a world that has the same greed for money, power, and selfish intentions, even in the church buildings. You see, everyone in the church building isn't necessarily living for or as the church in Christ. It is a religion, routine, practice, or just something to belong to for them, not a lifestyle. We're called to live for Christ, and we have to do so even when we're the only one standing in God's righteousness! We can't live for Christ and live like those who don't belong to Christ; we are called to live differently than the world. Jesus tells us the world won't like that we choose to live for Him; in fact, the world will hate us for it.

John 15:19 (NIV), If you belonged to the world, it would love you as its own. As it is, you do not belong to the world, but I have chosen you out of the world. That is why the world hates you.

We have power over the world, through Jesus Christ!

Don't be intimidated by the world!

We belong to Christ, so don't be intimidated by the world's hate and don't expect the world's love. You should expect for the world to mistreat you and be unfair in dealing with you, because you belong to Christ, and they mistreated Him first. If you find that you are expecting the world to do the right things, because you're misled by its deceptions, words, and false actions, test it. In every moment, challenge what you see, hear, and experience in the world against God's Word; challenge where you are! But, for you to stand firm for God in this world, you have to use the Word of God in every aspect of your life. That will require you to study His Word, pray for the understanding and revelation in His Word, and focus on His will for you! Know what He says in His Word or where to find it in His words, so that you aren't misled by the world's misuse or misunderstanding of His Word!

2 Timothy 2:15 (KJ21) 15 Study to show thyself approved unto God, a workman who needeth not to be ashamed, rightly dividing the Word of truth.

God has the power to change any and all things according to His will and plan. He can change you, if you truly desire to be changed and are willing to surrender to God. If you look at yourself and your relationship with God and desire more of Him, challenge where you are! God says, totally surrender to Him and His purpose, will, and plan for your life!

TELL GOD: "I WANT TO FEEL THE FIRE IN MY BONES!"

You are God's child, you're royalty! You are not
less than any other man! You are in God's likeness!

Chapter 4
Confidence In God!

Believe in God's power!

"I believe in God's power!" What a statement to make; now I must live it out before the world! There is a multitude of people that say they believe in God, but they live like He has no power. When things happen that activate our fears, we can allow the presence of fear to minimize God's power in our life. In life, trying times will find everyone, at some point. It doesn't matter who you are, what you have, who you know, or where you live, trials will find you. The question is, how do you deal with tribulation when it is sitting on your couch, in your living room? As believers in Christ, we should respond differently to tribulation than a non-believer in Christ; we respond with faith! Faith is not the absence of fear. Faith empowers you to live with a belief, in spite of the fear of what you see or don't see!

Hebrews 11:1-3 (NIV), Now faith is confidence in what we hope for and assurance about what we do not see. 2 This is what the ancients were commended for. 3 By faith, we understand that the universe was formed at God's command so that what is seen was not made out of what was visible.

God's power reaches far beyond what we see or can imagine. We cannot figure out God's mind, but we can believe in His power! Choosing to believe in God's power means we trust everything He says and does in, and through, His Word.

If God says it is, then it is!
If God says you can, then you can!
If God says He will, then He will!
If God said it, then it will do, be, and come to pass as
He said it will!

There is no greater power than the power of God, Christ, and the Holy Spirit! We have to also understand and believe that Satan has no power over us, unless we give him power. The only power he has is the power we choose to surrender to him. Jesus demonstrates this in the wilderness when Satan tried to tempt Him into acting on his deceptive promises.

Matthew 4:8-11 (NIV) 8 Again, the Devil took him to a very high mountain and showed him all the kingdoms of the world and their splendor. 9 "All this I will give you," he said, "if you will bow down and worship me." 10 Jesus said to him, "Away from me, Satan! For it is written: 'Worship the Lord your God, and serve him only" 11 Then the Devil left him, and angels came and attended him.

Jesus didn't give in to Satan's worthless promises; He used the Word of God and rendered him powerless to influence Him. We have the same authority and power to use God's Word to rebuke and reject whatever Satan has to offer. We have to believe, study it, and be ready and willing to use the power of the Word of God! Tell God: "I want to feel the fire in my bones!"

Thirst for God's Presence!

As you grow deeper, stronger, and wiser in God's Word, it will compel you to thirst for God's presence. We have the desire for so many things in the world, and we are willing to sacrifice the time, effort, energy, and money to obtain them. But, when it comes to our relationship with God, we often sell Him short in our effort to get more of Him. Take a moment and consider what we will go through to prepare for a date or to maintain a worldly relationship. I have taken risks, looked silly, been emotional; drove long distances, and even missed work for a relationship. However, when it came to God, I didn't take Him all that seriously. How about you? How have you dealt with God? If you're like me, you now realize how amazing, patient, and forgiving He is! Even when we had no interest in knowing Him, He loved, protected, blessed, covered, provided, and wanted us. What an amazing and awesome Savior! He loves us as filthy and selfish as we are when it comes to Him. We must learn from Jesus' example and chase after God's will and love, first and diligently. The question is, what are you willing to do for God to get what God has for you?

Matthew 6:33 "But seek first his kingdom and his righteousness, and all these things will be given to you as well."

God says to seek Him first and all these things will be given to you as well. As well implies that He's adding more. That means that He's already given to you before you even seek Him! In order to add something to your life, you have to have life first! When we think about everything God has given, is giving, and desires to give to us, how can we not thirst for His presence in our lives? Desiring to be in God's presence requires us to prepare ourselves. We have to clean up our lives with the blood of Christ, ask for forgiveness for our sins, constantly, and regulate our thoughts to Godly things. This is not easy, even for the seasoned believer, because we are always surrounded by the ways, thoughts, action, and things in a world that doesn't desire God! The more you desire God, the less you will desire the worldly things. Jesus talks about this with the woman at the well.

John 4:10-13 (NIV) 10 Jesus answered her, "If you knew the gift of God and who it is that asks you for a drink, you would have asked him, and he would have given you living water." 11 "Sir," the woman said, "you have nothing to draw with, and the well is deep. Where can you get this living water? 12 Are you greater than our father Jacob, who gave us the well and drank from it himself, as did also his sons and his livestock?" 13 Jesus answered, "Everyone who drinks this water will be thirsty again, 14 but whoever drinks the water I give them will never thirst. Indeed, the water I give them will become in them a spring of water welling up to eternal life."

The Samaritan woman didn't know who she was talking to, so she didn't understand what Christ was offering her. Desiring the things of the world will always leave you empty, but desiring God will fulfill everything in you! Jesus also made this clear while He was on the cross. For on the cross all of our sins were on Him. That means that at that time, our sins separated Him from God the Father, the living water. So, when Jesus said "I thirst," it wasn't a physical thirst, because He rejected what they offered Him. I believe He spoke these words and they thought He wanted water or wine, because He was at His worst. But they didn't understand that He had been separated from the living water and that He desired the presence of God, the Father, when He said the words "I thirst". If you want and need God's presence in your life and you want to desire less of this world, seek God, minute by minute! You have to thirst for God like a stranded man thirsting for water in the desert. Thirst for God's presence! Tell God: "I you want to feel the fire in my bones!"

Rely on God's provision!

As Jesus is speaking to the woman at the well, He's telling her about His ability to provide for her. He's saying that He will supply what she needs and that her life will never be the same. God has always provided for us. Even when we don't trust Him to provide, He does it! We have become so confident in ourselves and in what is developed in this world, that we lose sight of who's the source of our provision. Just because you have money, cars, education, good job, healthy habits, and know people in the world; doesn't make you the source of your provision! These things can lead you to think you are the god of your life, that you did it, and that you made it happen. Wrong! If you did it, tell me how you created the air you breathe, how you made your heartbeat, or how you woke up your mind this morning after being in a coma all night! We give ourselves too much credit, and we don't give God enough credit for who He is! You have to recognize that God is your source of life and begin to truly rely on God's provision. When you rely on God for what you need, you'll find peace in the middle of chaos, because you know God is in control. He controls the end result to everything. You can make choices, but God controls the result. According to John 1:1-4 (NIV) 1 In the beginning was the Word, and the Word was with God, and the Word was God. 2 He was with God in the beginning. 3 Through him all things were made; without him, nothing was made that has been made. 4 In him was life, and that life was the light of all mankind. 5 The light shines in the darkness, and the darkness has not overcome it.

Revelation 1:8 (NIV), "I am the Alpha and the Omega," says the Lord God, "who is, and who was, and who is to come, the Almighty."

This means that God is the creator of all things and He has the power to provide everything you need. Choose to rely on God's provision. Tell God: "I want to feel the fire in my bones!"

Rest in God's protection!

When you've accepted that God is your source of provision, you will realize that God is also your protector. You see, part of God's provision is His protection; He will protect you from Satan's efforts to destroy you. God doesn't want you to fear Satan, but God commands that you reverence Him as your protector and His absolute power.

Matthew 10:28 (NIV), Do not be afraid of those who kill the

body but cannot kill the soul. Rather, be afraid of the One who can destroy both soul and body in hell.

There are many in the world that won't take the war against Satan seriously, but we, as believers in Christ, know how serious it is. That is why we have to rest in God's protection. We can't battle the Devil with our fleshly ways and thoughts; we're too weak! We need the spirit, power, and strength of God to prevail over the Devil.

2 Corinthians 12:9 (NIV) But he said to me, "My grace is sufficient for you, for my power is made perfect in weakness." Therefore I will boast all the more gladly about my weaknesses, so that Christ's power may rest on me.

However, being under God's protection doesn't eliminate us from experiencing trials and tribulations. As stated earlier, we should expect trials and tribulation to come. Yes, the world will mistreat those who live for Christ, but that is also how God refines, grows, matures, and builds us in our trusting Him. Jesus tells us that trouble will come and that we shouldn't fear what happens, because He has power over these things. Our job is to rest in His protection and keep doing what He has created, called, and anointed us to do in this world.

When God allows tribulation,
It provides Devine motivation,
That gives you spiritual inspiration,
That will ignite a Holy determination,
That leads you to God's righteous elevation,
This places you at His designed destination!
Tribulation is God's way of training us for His elevation!

John 16:33 (NIV) "I have told you these things, so that in me you may have peace. In this world, you will have trouble. But take heart! I have overcome the world."

When you accept Christ as your savior, you're redeemed, covered, and empowered by the blood of Christ. The Holy Spirit lives in you, and you are under God's powerful protection. So, step into whatever God had called you to do, you do not have to wait on man's approval! God has already approved you the moment He chose you. Put aside everything that will hinder you from being what God says you are. There's a song that inspires me to seek more of God, and I listen to it over and over, so that the words live in me. The name of the song is "Different," by Micah Tyler, and my favorite lyrics are,

I wanna be different
I wanna be changed
'Til all of me is gone
And all that remains
Is a fire so bright
The whole world can see
That there's something different
So come and be different
In me

Jeremiah states "His word is in my heart like a fire, a fire shut up in my bones;"

Have confidence in God! Pray and ask God to ignite His spirit in you and to start a full blaze of fire in you, for Him!

TELL GOD: "I WANT TO FEEL THE FIRE IN MY BONES!!!!!!!"

No God, no me,
No Jesus, No way,
No Holy Spirit, No power!
God is!